ISBN-13: 978-1724859167
ISBN-10: 1724859161

Note:
Markers may bleed through on to the next page.
This is not a color by numbers, as you can see.
So, feel free to use any colors you want!
You can color in or outside of the lines.
There are no rules. Just try to relax
and do your own thing. Feel free to use
this page for testing out whatever
coloring instruments you're using. Or not.
It's your choice. Just color me now.